FOOTNOTE TO HISTORY

To Michael

MICHAEL HENRY

Footnote to History

Best wishes,

Michael

(October 2001)

London
ENITHARMON PRESS
2001

First published in 2001
by the Enitharmon Press
36 St George's Avenue
London N7 0HD

Distributed in Europe
by Littlehampton Book Services
through Signature Book Representation
2 Little Peter Street
Manchester M15 4PS

Distributed in the USA and Canada
by Dufour Editions Inc.
PO Box 449, Chester Springs
PA 19425, USA

ISBN 1 900564 27 0

British Library Cataloguing-in-Publication Data.
A catalogue record for this book is available
from the British Library.

Set in Bembo by Bryan Williamson, Frome,
and printed in Great Britain by
The Cromwell Press, Wiltshire

CONTENTS

This book celebrates the life of
Dennis Bennett-Jones (1910–95)
and is dedicated
to Tricia

Some of these poems have been previously published in the following
publications:
*Along the Line (Anthology, 1996); Cheltenham Poets 3; Distant Echo;
Giant Steps; Oxford Magazine; Poetry Nottingham; Poetry Review; Envoi;
Smiths Knoll; Staple; Stride; The Bridport Prize Anthology, 1993; Links;
The Interpreter's House; Other Poetry; The Writer's Voice; Weyfarers.*

Honour System and *Gentleman's Relish* appeared in *Lenten Visitor*
(KQBX Press, 1985).
Quarter Century Club and *Sitting Lessee* appeared in *Panto Sphinx*
(Enitharmon Press, 1991).

HORSES AT EDGE HILL STATION

I

Who had the measure of carters, carriers:
the callow ones and the cheapskates that tried
to telescope a three-horse load to two.

Who knew the Pythagoras of gradients
and were almost human about drayloads,
eyeing them up like an equine trade union.

Who breasted the steep slope of Tunnel Road
from a back-shantytown of coalman's wharves,
nostrils flaring like inverted funnels.

Carters whip them up the one-in-four,
then wipe the whip-marks off their behinds.
Against the bristle. Against the sweat.

Something holy about these horses.
Something of an industrial fiesta.

II

No jiggery-pokery. The real McCoy.
Horses jack-knifed wide onto the offside
straining sweat to make it up the steep slope,
halting traffic with their draught.
Whoa! I saw the carters
soothe away the leashmarks of their lashes
like calamine lotion to a cut
and the horses nuzzle 'thank-you'.

9

I ignored the policeman's beckoning
and waited truant for the next relay
freighted like ships with teak and damascene.
My satchel weighted with dead textbooks
I spat out a breakfast tomato seed
imagining pomegranate.

THE FIRST CRUSADE

They told me God was like the light
that walked through panes of glass. They said
prayers blew across the ethereal plain
and faith had the power to move a mountain.
God was classified in their house.
How they fought against the disbelief
that etched a shadow on my small boy's face.

They tried to drag me to their mountain
and starve my apostasy out
with gruel and soapy water by the glass.
I watched the light play snakes and ladders
with the shadow until they shut it out
with clerical plain black curtains
and listened to their prayers where family came first.

HONOUR SYSTEM

He was a non-denominational
and worked an honour system
we could worship where we pleased –
on Sundays on the oak-settle in the hall
he left a roll of coppers
for our collection money
graduated according to our growth –
and if we failed to take our pile
the older we were the taller the reproach –
and as for misappropriation of the funds
it happened once
the crime uncovered and the culprit ushered upstairs –

he confronted me in his study
from where he'd pointed out the heights of Liverpool
two cathedrals the Liver Building and a University to aspire to –
molelike I looked down at the taupe carpet –
from taupe to tawny just a handful of words in the dictionary
but how far a remove
from the tawny amber light
that streamed in through the window
as if my missing coppers were molten in the sunset.

RED CURRANT JELLY

My parents practised child rotation:
the youngest was always mother's pet,
the second youngest father's favourite.

The war-prints in his waiting-room
by Lady Butler R.A.
were hung like stations of the cross.

Six of them. And six of us.
Scotland For Ever was my brother's
but *Quatre Bras*, the bloodiest, was mine.

'Red Currant Jelly' we called it,
tiptoeing on our voices,
woozy from the smell of musketry.

At meal-times he'd come back from theatre
with pinheads of brittle blood
on the Paris goblets of his glasses.

My sisters pushed their plates aside
but I smeared onto muttonfat
my knife's thumbprint of red jelly –

something precious like a stamp.

CHELSEA PHYSIC GARDEN

London's secret garden
walled and sunken like a close.

He showed us Ophelia's patch:
samples of rosemary and rue,
hyssop, lovage, lemon balm.

He dispensed his own
herbs culinary and medicinal:
foxglove, *digitalis* in dog-eared
doctor's Latin, hand on heart
like Bonaparte.

Systematic order beds of dropwort,
beeplants for dyestuffs and perfumery,
eau de Cologny mint and clary:
two seeds in water
smoke out a mucilage.

Rock Garden from Mount Hecla,
here he did his 'Iron Man',
burnet, darnel, plants of après Agincourt.
Agrimony, hellebore,
escapees like Bruce's spider.

And narcissus poeticus –
his memory's buttonhole.

LEX TALIONIS

So nearly a death on the kitchen table
an appendectomy with his father's
ether and chloroform bag of smells –
the boy became a surgeon of inanimate objects
unpicking the anatomy of suits
whose hessian interfacing had such a German feel –

slim magpie pickings
when the kestrels have feasted
scrabbling for the rag and bones
the talon in the velvet glove . . .

they were playing rhyme-around-the-table
'the cheese and the women were pukka
we were ahead in the first chukka . . .'
the buck as always stopped with him
pétanque . . . he could have knocked their blocks together
the men so stiff-lapelled
the women in balaclava hairdos . . .

they wanted to suppress him like an electrical gadget
so he wouldn't cause interference . . .
the sashcord was hanging down
looped like a pendulum of death.

A GLASS-STOPPERED BOTTLE

Whenever I touch this bottle
summeriness, like dandelions,
rubs off on my fingers;
seeds snowstorm. A glass horseshoe
is brailled into the base
like a coat of arms.

I look through the equator
of its slack yellow transparency,
that stoppered air bubble
or topsy-turvy spirit level
contradicting Galileo,
turning my round world flat.

If I unstoppered it, unbound
the mummy-cloth layers round the neck,
would I fall into dry oblivion
from ether, from chloroform
or simply recoil
from the essence of flowers?

I have taken your instruments
and your way of life to auction.
Were they your one true identity?
A different love this,
lingering on in a half-life
where grainstones of glass jewelesce . . .

I wanted something for nothing,
Murano instead of surgical glass.
To scrape out with a curette
the fruit from the fluid,
to tap on the glass
with obstetric fingers . . .

HOUSE OF DOCTORS

Last thing at night
as other men might walk the dog
my father rolled up his sleeves
and rubbed and dubbed the davenport
from his cousin's vicarage
until it shone like fiddleback.

I hear him addressing the grandfather clock
if its complexion didn't come up as new.
Another Celtic spit on cloth
saw doctors' faces reflected in the wood:
his children's and his children's children.

And first thing in the morning
I see him climb a leaning curve up the stairs,
polishing the banister with his sleeve,
snagging it gently on the hoops
that bound the rail like wedding bands.

'Llanberis, Cader Idris . . .'
mumbling the magical Welshness of names,
reading the day's sheaf
of doctor's telegrams,
greeting his reflection like a brother.

'Hello, Tom!' to pinstripes,
morning coat and carpet slipper
tiptoeing *fianchetto*
across the parquet floor.
His dark shadow disappears

into the consulting room where curtains flutter
patterns of sunshine and shade
and light comes streaming in,
in thin crosses of watery waves.
Even the light in a brilliant white coat.

MY GRANDFATHER'S SCALPEL

Your beautiful tortoiseshell scalpel,
more like a lady's set of combs,
retractable
as one of childhood's
remembered pocket-knives.

I set my thumbnail in the notch
and open up a billhook blade,
my forefinger
runs along to draw
a thought bubble of blood.

I see it in your waistcoat pocket
as you drive the surgeon on a late-night case,
sidelights
like tiny torches peering down
the throat of blacked-out Liverpool.

Or cracking open the shell
to beat first half then a whole
raw egg
into my late-night feed,
the blood-bud on my finger

the issue of all those bloodshot eggs,
the marbling on the tortoiseshell
come true.

PIGEONS OF HAFODYMYN

I

He housed them on the balcony
in a dovecot of wooden girders
sawn with his father's medical saw.
Tumblers he liked best: Red Arrow birds
that looped the blue fantastic.

He tongue-and-grooved the joints and made
wire pigeon–flaps that flipped open
from outside. Then snapped to, trapped.
White fantails he could never breed
or jacobins. Just commoners.

He took his birds to flying school.
Hunger, he found, was the homing factor.
He started them on little
hungry flights. He was their stringmaster
pulling avian vapour trails.

And when the birds became too much,
his father took them to Hafodymyn
where Cousin Peg and pretty Nan
were waiting in their Welsh Sunday best.
They set the pigeons loose.

II

Bonfires of driftwood burn along
the tideway. Rubble-burning, river stubble-burning.

I remember we used to say: 'Never
throw even a twig into a busy river.'

Rings of blue smoke curl into the air. Pigeons
peck up the grits and grains.

I wonder could their forebears by any chance
be the ones, Hafodymyn's.

MERCHANT IVORY POEM

Merchant Ivory would get it right:
leafing through *The Lady* 1924
to a furnished holiday cottage at Penrose.
The detail of non-detail: no bed linen.
Sea-air bracingly medicinal.

The seven seater open Berliet
steepling down the country lanes
its speediest way to shore.
Luggage on a rack at the back.
Between the wings. On running boards.

The *Boy's Own* elder brother. Slightly bald.
The girls face to face. Like a Scottish reel
steepling down the country lanes
rubbernosing through glades of honeysuckle
to the deep blue tartans of the sea.

Wall-to-wall sunshine. Day by day.
Cornish waters. Pastis clear.
The playful tide coming in like a parent
setting up his son's Hornby Double 0 trainset
on Christmas Eve. Or is that an anachronism?

I can see them clean as print.
Smiling happily at time.

TRAIN BAND, 1930

The train red-noses into a tunnel
seems to hold its steamy breath
at a signal from a band of boys.

In that sudden black-out
they shin up the backs of seats
clamber through the scramblespace
between compartments . . .

Scene-change flat in thirty seconds!

They sit cool as choirboys on pew
while pepper-and-salty gents with newspapers
gape goggle-eyed
at these coming-out-of-the-tunnel visions.

Newspapers, tunnels, darkness, ghosts . . .
Little did they know! Little did they know!

WORLD'S END, CLWYD

Where the moors are blistered blue with bilberries
and the heather feathers up a startled bird.
Where every clump covers a grouse or partridge.
Ruabon Mountain, Esclusham Mountain,
Gribin Pass, the hamlet of Menira
and like an English amen, World's End.

Where I drink in the cool drops of evening
after a day travelling in the coupé
with windows closed and aunts worrying
about the pinkness of their complexion.
Where the moon glows like the light in a railway carriage
on a night sleeping out at the end of the world.

Where tomorrow I will meet up with my life at Menira.

THE LIEUTENANT'S ACCOUNT

After a hard night's billeting
at the Olympia, cheek by jowl
in its vast claustrophobic cavern,
we lined the streets at Whitehall.

Foot-marched, as the charabancs
were on strike. Somehow the British public
didn't want all this, coming
so soon after the Abdication.

On the way we passed water
naval fashion, even numbers, odd,
retching from the Foreign Office reek
of raw undiluted whisky.

Peacocking the pageantry,
tops of our hats glistening like icing,
we glimpsed a white princessly arm
leaning out of its carriage-window.

No newsreels. No Pathé Pictorials.
Just fitting into the paradescape.
Our sisters standing in Park Lane,
tickets buckshee from the Shipping Office.

It was a cold coronation.
Ashes of roses on the 12th of May,
in the very quick of summer.
Just the best time of the year.

FOR THE MISSING

I dream at night I've missed the marble lists:
the thousand platelets cracked in Menin Gates.
I dream of someone shouting out whose fists
bang at the cosy comfort of my dates.

I ask whose tumbrils these, whose scullion's prams
that throw out shadows of a future war.
I dream I'm taking notes and sit exams
forgetting all that I'm remembering for.

I watch the raindrops tinting bracken mauve
and pools of redness spill along the road.
I watch the frosty spider's webs that wove
a shroud of lace around each heavy load.

I'll send them Interflora for their grave.
England, daughter-rich and poor and brave.

SUMMER OF THIRTY-NINE

I

That dangerous summer
when swallows minimed telephone wires
with bars of *Horst Wessel Lied* . . .
my mother and her sisters
hired bikes at Hanover, then Goslar,
then Hildesheim with the pretty name
where Sheila refused to say 'Heil Hitler!'

That brochure blueness of eye and sky
those hutments off the beaten track
the anaesthetic playing of violins . . .
Kathleen left a German fiancé.

'Handle with Care!' those piecrust promises
as England was shock-frozen out of summer.
'We must share and sacrifice our all!'
my mother rises to a rousing speech
offers up her double bed, turns red
to catcalls of male applause.

II

A wadi burst like a water pipe:
pools of rainwater – earth's fontanelles.
I am tired and indisposed like Wordsworth
from 'walking in the wood composing . . .'

As I think of that dangerous summer
an overhanging branch combs my hair,
blood juices on my rolled-up arm
and my heart beats battle-faster.

I like it when the flesh is fretted
and the raw pheromones break out.

III

Plus ça change, plus c'est la même chose.
The wind page-turns the burning books
cyclostyles the hectic in the leaf.

THE WEALTH OF POLAND

25th August 1939

The *Wealth of Poland*
draws out of harbour, charges
into the white horses
of a once German sea.

Three boats, two British
and one German escort.

I'm doing what I've been trained to do,
Royal Naval Volunteer Reservist
serving on one of the British boats.
Lightning forks the subfusc like a wild silk tie,
a box of them in my cabin.

As the *Wealth of Poland*
draws into Scottish port
its German escort blows out
farewell funnels of smoke.

Something tells me
I'm going to be prejudiced against collaborators.

25th August 1943

How can I convince
this German Jew he's vulnerable
for all the German tree-rings in his bones?
Geneva Convention is just a game we play.

We know there's something smoking.
Is it the doctor with the sleazy ties
who tries to turn brown eyes to green,
injects some bloodshot in each eye?

Something tells me
I've been one of the luckier ones.

Faded is the wealth of Poland,
faded as that labyrinthine rose.

MATTERS OF NO SMALL IMPORTANCE

The German guns' poum! poum!
cures would-be peeping toms.
I slide the flap
of the boat-turret back . . .

Fall into long-deprivated slumber –
forty-eight hours from Pompey Harbour
to Henry V's Harfleur . . . Taken
awake at St. Valéry-en-Caux . . .

Have a *temp job* operation
at the field dressing station . . .
Freighted onto a cattle truck,
trans-shipped onto lorry-back,

ricketed along tortuous roads . . .
Over-ripeness, half-asleepness,
apple-logs smoulder in the para-dark.
I recognise the lorry marque.

'My father had a Berliet!'
'*Ça ne fait rien*. Does it matter?'
a wounded Frenchman mutters.
Yes, it matters. Every day.

CIVILISATION

Two hours at Monet's Gare Saint Lazare.
Even a station's an oasis to a prisoner,
mothers with shopping baskets pushing pushchairs,
children cuffing one another,

sunflowers klieg-eyed from the light. The world
scratching its innocent lottery card.
In war one loses touch with such humanities.
Never had I wanted to escape so hard.

Spain was risky but Portugal, I'd heard, was safe.
I'd cast my crutches off into the Seine,
sleep rough like a snake that had escaped
and live off the golden windfalls of the sun.

DOVER'S POWDER

Depression mopes across Germany.
Prisoners huddle as rugby players do.
Behind me the foul fumette of cell,
ahead I tread the long hard road to Marburg
weighted down now by the stones I've lost . . .

The hospital is like a gay gymnasium club.
The German doctor wants only smiley boys
has them undress in open-plan cubicles
X-rays their privates in a shoe machine
for little operations or 'slittings'.

The expert experimenting into eyes
squints into the playschool blue of my iris
attaches a new head on an auriscope
then probes as for an auricular confession
into the cold tympanum of my ear.

The hospital canteen is divided up
like a dim-lit bookshop with foreign sections:
there are Frenchmen breaking bread at both ends
and Russkies, Russkies, the last people . . .
My voice goes squeaky when I try to speak.

And stranger still an English hospital matron
with a mitred lampshade on her hair
waiting on me with egg and Marmite soldiers.
I feel her cuffs strigil down the sharp of my back
and see the white cliffs of Dover powdered on her face.

NUMBER 77 D.S.C.

The sun rakes through an avenue of poplars
as we march to Marburg in prisoners' subfusc.
A snow-white nurse receives us at the camp.

They expose the varicose tracery of my parts
pink as the underside of a dockleaf.
I fear they're going to sterilise us.

The sun begins to set a Samian red.
My mates are in a good mood – wild tarmac fellows –
I've got nothing against them for their strong
swallowing gulps but it's lowering
to think we might be fed on human flesh.

Instead of the meat I refuse to eat
I get extra *Kartoffel* and bread.
Cabbages grow like cones on pine-trees.
Someone's robbed me of my German rye,
I eye each suspect in the picnic ranks.

This is Märchen country – Brothers Grimm.
I get my bread back from the leader
of a drove of jobbing dwarves and spend
much of my young manhood weeping.

BREAKING THE CODE

You want to know what it was like
being lost, being an 'air person'.

I'll tell you. Like a fly cobwebbed in barbed wire.
When I asked for Hugo's 'German Words'
all I got was 'Nein, nein!'
And when I asked for needle and thread
'Deutsch sprechen!' their beadling retort.

My German captors thought they were being clever.
Threadneedle? Bank of England? See.
Job-shadowed by another Hugo,
my counterpart, a German shipping clerk,
we had to be as close as this. Like twins.

I'm telling you the censored truth.
We were fed and housed like cattle
on our milk round of the prison camps.
And there was an odour of petshops.

PARAPHRASING CHURCHILL

We thought it would be a kindness to kill her.
Her mother and father were already dead.
The building was like a Dutch barn.
And her brother in the cookhouse too.
Her whole family. Nothing to live for.
You didn't agree.

When the naked Jewish girl
came running out like a rabbit
you ducked her down in the split-trenches.
Her body was wisped with albino hairs
and her face was intensely pale.
She should have gone to ballet classes
with your little Degas nieces.

You'd been with us three years maybe four.
Refractory, you never spoke our language.
How could you learn so little in so long.
Your leg wired up in a Thomas splint,
the ankle skewered like a piece of meat
with rabbit's bone to let it drain.
That wound has got to heal from inside out.

BLACKOUT

I have your letter, a birth in Le Mans,
that light in the blackout
that didn't have to be extinguished

in spite of German officers at the door.
Verdunkelt – their word for it
spits out like a swear.

Black tar-papered windows trap
Auspuff of prisoners' breath,
undercover cigarette smoke.

I take my mattress outside.
The balcony is ten by six.
The stars are not *verdunkelt*

and the night feeds me
frühschoppen of fresh air
making up for missing meals.

I try to hold your shadow tight,
loosen up the straps
like the rigging of a ship.

THE CARD-PLAYERS

If you had seen them, Cézanne clones,
chaffing as they roughed a spade.
Or heard their chatter. Einsteins
of relativity, lots
of ready talk but nothing heavy.
Or smelt their rolled-on Rizla breath,
bartering for fag-ends, toilet paper.

Card-players coped best in prison-camps.
Mock-mercenary about their chips
and cards hallowed in their dirt. Great
Caesar would have had such men about him,
packs in tunic pockets preserving them
from the rifle shot of boredom.

COMMONPLACE BOOK

Sunday, 23rd October –
'There are no atheists in foxholes.'

Leafleted with propaganda
driven like a Jehu across Deutschland
c/o POW camp Langdorf
its pylon-high parameters
strongholded with pill-boxes.

Monday, 24th October –
'All anarchists must wear a tie.'

Heil Hitler! tongues shoot out
bayonet-wet with spittle.
Firing off a loose cannon of dissent
I echo *Morgen früh! Morgen früh!*
sub-Dylan Thomas across the valleys.

Tuesday, 25th October –
'Life is war and war is life.'

'*Viel lange* I've been *Kriegsgefangene.*'
A Gerry with overhanging upper lip
wants me please to sign the visitors' book
and attest the purity of my line.
My signature straddles volumes of descent.

Wednesday, 26th October –
'A million deaths is a statistic,
but one death is a tragedy.'

I wanted a burial at sea
riding the vanilla-crested waves
popping like a roasted chestnut.
Pin-up princesses wall my mind
babies gurgling with sheer satisfaction.

25th November my sell-by date –
POW bread still sitting heavy on the stomach
sextons dig up the silence of my mind.

DICING FOR MARKS

A split nail in the perfect smile of teeth
suave and civilised as cyanide.

A squeegee voice-box
that wheedles like a dentist's drill.

The Deputy Führer wants to release me
as if I were a bird.

I see the bloom on his glasses
and Scotland in a far-off lens.

The heat seeps through moth-eaten fatigues
cooks me till the flesh comes off the bone.

He leans back on his shooting-stick
like a monk on a misericord.

....

Führer and Deputy
two postage stamps *se tenant*.

In the cells we dice for prisoner-of-war marks
and Geneva grounds for repatriation

as we summer out the [∞] airless days
in Treysa and in Langdorf.

ROMMEL ROULETTE

I watched a white light of swallows
swooping under the bridge
and felt the electricity flow.

Why didn't the field marshal shoot me?
Firing to the right of me,
firing to the left of me,
the stream of bullets clicked past.

Arms crossed like a pair of dividers,
the hairs on my neck at attention,
I'd given my word not to escape
which I hoped would shoot wide of the mark.

HOSPITAL PASS

Where is this place? I'm told
Whiston, near Liverpool. An old
workhouse hospital,
and I'm *schwerverwundet*,
in the first prisoners to be invalided out.

Who is this woman visitor?
Like a cat with a following of toms.
She's been told I've seen her son.
I say, 'So many prisoners . . .'
like rabbits in the grass.

Do I remember seeing him?
His missing person's number, his name?
I saw him as a prisoner of war.
I remembered him from way before.
Playing rugby, three quarter. Yes,

I saw her son *verwundet*, feigning madness
to be categorised a hopeless case.
Dicing her mother's fear for
my prisoner's eyes, trying to *home* me
with some Red Cross fags . . .

Couldn't she be a little less . . .
Couldn't she leave me to a kinless priest, dressed
for a Pardon in neutral grey.
What more can I say?
That I left my godless heart out there
and got away.

JUMP SUNDAY

A dads' day-out, in hats, and suits
with hankie in breast pocket.
Such an entry into Aintree it was,
like Palm Sunday before Easter.
Touring the course with kids,
dispensing racing lore:
'Here's where so-and-so fell.'
'Best place to take her's from the right
at Becher's Brook,' where dad doffed his cap.
I almost saw an equine Fosbury Flip
clear the bars of such a jump.

Later, billeted at Aintree in the stables,
such an esprit de corps it was.
Ours sported a double winner: Reynoldstown
in Thirty-five and Thirty-six.
We jumped to attention,
out-jumping other stables
and at night we dreamed of a giant horse
clearing the bars of Dunkirk,
taking Arnhem from the right.
At night we dreamed of Reynoldstown
before our Easter at the front.

CORPORAL VIOLET

She read over an untouched breakfast
that you'd been reported 'missing'.

She read about the small coasting vessel
that ran hard and fast ashore and how
her gallant actions were the talk of many.
It could have been the morning paper.

She read the list of men in your command:
Sub Lieutenant Pryor and Carpenter,
familiar to her now as household words.

She followed in finger-pilgrimage
the keel-taps of your little ship
and circled place-names on her map:
St. Valéry-en-Caux, Veules-les-Roses.

She's worn a violet come the violet season
like a corporal for her lost Napoleon.

DISTRESSED BRITISH SEAMAN

I

You begin to suss out their routine:
how they check you in to check you out
and shunt you *intourist* from camp to camp.

They delouse you in a massive bath
with a wooden lid to trap in heat
and a hole to put your head through like the stocks.

You test the water with your wrist
anticipating a moment's bliss.
You slither in against a weight of fur,

an otter going for that airhole round your neck.
A hand fends it off your testicles.
Your flesh which should turn warm turns cold.

II

You've sussed out rules for repatriation
and you're sitting on deck in the Baltic,
beard trimmed to a matchstick length,

your history rolled up behind you in the wash
with Rügen on your left and that grand-
paternal figure of Sweden in the offing.

You're smoking your last Red Cross ration
when you see the tail-fin of a warship
and 'shit' becomes a reflexive verb again.

IMPLEMENTS OF WAR

I

He told me how
he was taken at St. Valéry,
then onto Rouen, then Forges-les-Eaux
where he surrendered his effects
except a French school atlas
and his compass: North, North by East,
North North East, North East by North . . .
how he boxed the compass, keeping
up the practice just in case . . .

He told me how
he studied the Geneva small print
at Kloster Heina where the Germans
had pinned a copy on the wall:
preamble, clauses, he knew them all by rote.
How he pawned his atlas and his compass
when he knew he could be shot for less
because the *Feldwebel* had such an honest head,
double crown like two plugholes in the bath.

II

After the trading-in of prisoners
I watched him write to the *Feldwebel*
at his new address in North America,
asking for his atlas and his compass back,
his confiscated 'implements of war'.
It was impossible.

I watched as other cards came in:
'Peace and goodwill to all men'.
Where was the *Feldwebel* then?
Tucking into a haunch of venison
or snowshoeing in a red light district of hawthorn?
West North West.

S-BLOCK

Now the prisoner winters out the war,
now the quartermaster counts his store.

Now the Jerries are doing jankers,
the officers and other rankers.

Soon the Lancaster will have flown
its cockleshell of heroes home.

And R-Block that housed ten thousand men
is a histogram of huts again.

Now only the Russians in S-Block
drag out their lives, poor sods, in hock.

RINGING THE BELL WITH A 'D'

I

Repatriated, he fills in
the debriefing questionnaire:
Are you a war-wounded? Yes.
Were you treated humanely?
He doesn't want to answer 'yes',
he doesn't want to answer 'no'.

Plumes plucked like a Christmas capon,
he passes through the sword-edged shrubbery
and rings his first initial in morse
dong ding ding on the doorbell,
expecting his parents' faces
to light up two hundred watts of joy.

An eleven-month old grandchild
is performing an African wardance
on the bars of its playpen
and dribbling HIS 'red ration' of egg
like a toothpaste tube of yellow paint.
Do you like your new nephew?

He doesn't want to answer 'yes',
he doesn't want to answer 'no'.

II

Roses withered in the heat,
noses snuffled in their sleep.
This little pig went to war.

The baby plays on a sea of sand
mottled like a thrush's throat.
This little pig was a prisoner.

. He turned into the gaunt moralising
old wolf of Aesop's fable.
This little pig came home.

He taught the baby to bend
the wooden bars of its playpen.
One little pig against imprisonment.

An angel led him
down the roseblown streets.
This little pig went free, free, free.

DEMOB SUIT HERO

I

It wasn't a bit like the poster:
soldier returning to tickertape welcome,
blouse-and-skirt wife tripping out
with little boy in stockings and garters.

It was like Shakespeare's seventh age of man:
sans battledress, sans greatcoat,
sans kitbag, compass and firearms,
and forage cap that made their hairline recede.

They could've done with a bit
of the governor's panache –
best cutter in Bold Street, renowned
for the unsewn label on his clothes.

Wearing utility suits
the old boy would've spat on
they needed a medal or two
like a drayhorse craves brasses.

But this was history being unmade.
And a proverb in the pulled cracker of their mind:
'He who knows no history
is condemned to repeat its disasters.'

II

I'd sooner be a tourist than a hero
if I had a suitcase to pack up and go.

I'm agoraphobic from the spaces
of these tall-ceilinged rooms and terraces.

In every white light I see a bomber's moon
and scream into the reflection of my doom.

I write patriotic letters to The Times:
'Homes fit for heroes, heroes fit for homes.'

I styptic-pencil in each stubbled wound
and hover round the lobbies, dressing-gowned.

Is this the England that I left and loved,
did three years prison for and quietly grieved?

GENTLEMAN'S RELISH

With gifts of gold and frankincense and myrrh
his family welcomed him back into the fold –
Oxford marmalade for breakfast
and coffee with cream and demerara sugar –
his favourite flavour of crystalline fruits
afternoon tea in the drawing room
with best bib and tucker on
and 'Auntie Macassar' on the chairs
but he was anti childish jokes –
sandwiches pasted together with gentleman's relish
and mustard – no he didn't like the khaki taste
his was the senior service –

he had a number
P.O.W.'d in black ink on his towels –
they'd given him a Gieves' suit
with proper cuff-buttons that unbuttoned
and booked him with a specialist in Rodney Street –
but no he refused to go –
the German doctor had patched him up like new –
now that he was free – free at last
the returned gentleman
didn't relish flying his phantom flag
for their convenience.

LULWORTH SKIPPER

For us this is
the wrong half of the correspondence.

*'Dear Skipper: I hope you don't mind
the familiar form of address.'*

We see you through the eyes of your Scottish corporal,
swinging along, your leg supported by string from your neck.

*'Dear Skipper: I assure you any help
I may have been was a pleasure to perform.'*

'Skipper.' So that was what
everyone called you in Rouen.

Dear Skipper: We see you faltering
mothlike towards the light.

'Chequered, cloudy, dingy, Lulworth, pearl.'
The letter warms each reading like a fire opal.

HONESTY BOX

After the prison darkness, the Hôtel Dieu,
after the darkness of the D'Ernemont convent,
now the darkness of a railway carriage
with blinds fitting more than flush
on blackened window-pane surrounds.

He lifted up a corner of the blind
like scraping away ice in winter, saw
a shaving mirror view of Moselle vineyards,
the first he'd ever seen; and then remembered
the Picards and their gift of sweet white grapes:

> *Jean who'd dared to paint Monet's cathedral,*
> *Françoise with her young girl's half-moustache*
> *as if Nature were punning on her hormones;*
> *the entente cordiale of their Christmas party*
> *where juggler's plates made do for lack of food . . .*

Supposed to be *en route* for Switzerland
the train turned to ecclesiastical north
and stopped at Metz where he counted
forty-three dead leaves lying in state
like the shreds of his Swiss world . . .

'How dare you mumbo jumbo out the window!'
a Gerry face, angry, Germolene pink.
Would have been in deep trouble but
all the resistance in the train
opened their window-blinds . . .

                                    . . . Now sitting
at another window-seat, slips
our French boy a small *pourboire*:
an honesty box from the war.
He hadn't had a bad war up till Metz.

54

FRANCISCAN UNCLE

He was Rembrandt's Franciscan friar in the flesh
a single bed-sit for a cell –
intravenoused to the radio
on even days he read the *Morning Post* –

He suffered us little children
treated us to the latest in Italian ice cream
pistachio rum and raisin
but for himself a bland vanilla blend –

As we grew up
he grew more glum than glad to see us
reluctant to break the enclosure
of his solitary order –
yet when we stood up to go
he'd hold us hovering hour long at the door
in the catch-22 of outstayed welcome
and premature departure.

WELSH TWEED

Something about his old Welsh tweed
the deep rufous 'rough' inside the lapel
hard and coarse as builder's sand

something more than the vintage
of his prima donna dressing gowns
and suits of pyjamas in light blue
with white piping

even something about his DIY patches
the crosshatching of receding grey chevrons
and the beading MOT leather . . .

But mostly about
his inside pocket that still buttoned
and the personalised name-tag
liveried in red
like a Rolls Royce radiator emblem
before his world's mourning began.

HOUSE CHARGE

There is no cover charge in libraries.
At ease he leafs through *Country Life* and *Field*:
High Society hot properties for sale
and a wedding up in Bayswater.

Once he'd had an address in Prince's Square,
been pictured with a princess on H.M. Hebe.
Cup-bearer to the gods, flying
like a burgee before the mast.

From there to the small print of charter parties,
clerking for the shipping-line 'Hadjilias'.
From H.M. Hebe to Hadjilias,
from ancient to demotic Greek.

He takes another peek inside and sees
the print-white napery and plates
of equilateral sandwiches folded over
thin as paper napkins.

Then picks up a more lightweight paper,
scans the classified *Miss Lonelyhearts*.
Stacks *Country Life* and *Field* back in the racks.
Can't afford the house charge of that club.

NO NEED TO LET US KNOW

He gets out at the rebuilt station,
walks a short distance along Duke Street,
tipsy from the whiff of frosted spray,
staggering like a steamboat on the Clyde.

In the feathery seeds of old man's beard
he sees a woman's dishevelled hair
and in the frosted haws ice-pink lips,
reminding him of pleasures he has missed.

He turns up Haresfield Avenue
and there's his niece opening the door,
saying he's just in time for lunch
and the family all at table, glasses charged,

rising with 'Uncle! Uncle!' as if it were a grace.

DISTANT RELATIVE

How did he manage to do it?
Wizarding out of memory
and a filing system of brown envelopes
those twenty-year old letters
from a third cousin in 'Rhodesia'
with those beautiful blue stamps
he wanted to accuse of vagueness
antelope head on a field of azure
and the flowering pink menorah
that might have been a jacaranda plant.

How did he manage to do it?
Setting my mind at rest in the distance
with a PO Box Number
somewhere in Chisipite or Banket
and those beautiful blue stamps
from childhood philately.

HOUSEWIFE

First aid pack for inanimate things:
needle, thread, buttons, safety pins.

Domestic science teacher in miniature
that sutures up old Thirties shirts

on borrowed thread, on borrowed time
and the small print of what might have been.

A feminist *avant la lettre*,
a housewife in the second sense.

PHANTOM BRIDE

Without spouse or live-in companion –
even my Guernsey milk jugs are a pair
one coppery sun, one lunar silver . . .

sometimes to forget I go to light opera
but though I sit near the orchestra
I'm too shy to look up at the bride

when she sings, hums or mimes her duet
to that face in the front of the stalls . . .
the show is on tour in the provinces

so I write to my deceased cousin's sons
for I have acquaintance in every port
and tell them of the love in my eyes . . .

then when my stage bride sings or just hums
it's as if I've willed them my eyes
imparted a new texture to sound . . .

snug as a dormouse in a clergy house
my heart aglow like a coal effect fire
my Guernsey milk jugs all of a pair.

REPLENISH THE EARTH

When I went to my sister's wedding with Syd,
both on leave from our squadrons,
the division was an upstairs, downstairs one.

But now I keep getting reminded in church
I haven't been fruitful and replenished the earth,
the division's a geometrical one,
dividing my savings into wedding gifts
for great nieces and great nephews.

Above the London traffic he hears
the wheezing voices of starlings
and he envies them their wings
and their many multiplications
like sycamore seeds

floating aimlessly down
to earth.

BADGES IN THE SNOW

'Small guilts assume mammoth proportions.'

This morning had to go out
to the shop before breakfast.
The snow was driven hard
and not yet trampled on.
Followed the same track back.
'Où sont les neiges d'antan?'
Saw my heels had trodden in
the imprint of a line of badges.

Winter 1920. Cook's badge.
Failed to make an open fire.
Dad, practical as ever,
fried my bacon indoors.
I got booted out of Scouts
for only owning up belatedly.
Still tenderfoot, 'Je ne regrette rien.'
The air crisps with campfire cooking.

LOBB'S FARM

It's like a Constable painting:
everyone helps.
The farmer cuts corn
in ever-decreasing circles
skittling rabbits into the stubble.

A small boy and his brother
pick them out of the stacks;
the brother wrings their necks like jacktowels,
holding them dead by the ears like Spanish onions.
Kind Farmer Lobb comforts a sister
who's been struck by a spade on the chin.

I hear the horse's hooves striking
'three halfpence and two pence'
in the currency of the day
and have to duck my head
to become so small,
rubbing the past from my eyes.

LET IT STAND

Stettin was German to the very boot.
For four years we prisoners
prospered our private petty war,
boasted of losses, not success.
They tried to make us German then,
to strain our Englishness through cheesecloth.
We had to hate to survive.

It was only after
clocking back to England, English time,
that batteries turned off turned on again
with a sickly convalescent charge.
The streets are strewn with broken glass.
Like blossom. One of us traced out
with his boot: *Stettin stet.*

Stettin whose imprimatur has disappeared
in the liveried letters of a Polish name.

SLOW TRAIN TO LIME STREET

The stopping train starts
with an agitation of wheels.
I make instinctively for the middle
from the days when trains
waggled their cat's-tails
and belched halitosis.

In the middle carriages
I feel as safe and anonymous
as a number in brackets.

DEAD SEA SCROLLS

We walk along the sandflats
to where a sandmartin and her baby
are hiding in the cliff.
We follow him through mist,
follow him through sadness
but lose him in the saltings
and the martins in a grain of sand.

The lettering nib feet of birds
have left lines of script along the sand
and we can see him
toeing over seashells from the past:
Here's roundhand for you, here's roundhand oblique.

We lift the mist of tracing paper
from an old photograph album
and read roundhand lines of writing:
Fisherman's Cove, Sunny Cove, Waterford Farm.

CABARET

The man in Number Twenty-two
loves the louche austerity
of a black-and-white French film
and its lattice gates
that open and close
like demi-monde dance routines.

The woman in Number Thirty-four
admires herself in the burnished brass plates
and the walnut finish that glisters
like the vernissage on old cars.

But for him, living on the top floor,
it is a play in four acts.
Sally Bowles lit a cigarette
and Orson Welles squeezed into such a lift.

They want to install
a state-of-the-art lift
that would give residents vertigo.
He has mounted a round-the-clock vigil,
finger on the red seal button.

MOVING

I

'It's got two missing springs, I'm afraid.'
His landlord who'd played Charley's Aunt in rep
auditioning from the cast-iron bed
twisted an unexpected card of honesty.

The room was *mise en scène* with period props:
majolica glazed like a bacon flitch,
a shade of fruit on a side-table,
two sea-urchins and a scrumpled shell.

But it was the chestnut leaning against the window,
chintz-pink and green, that carried the candle.
Chestnut, hawthorn and scattering cherry
that every year would reinvent confetti.

II

Nicotine stains where his pictures were:
'Eviction', 'Beauty Bathing in Cairngorm Waters'.
Glazing-bars chop up the vista from the studios,
glass-fronted bookcases where the curtains were.

He opens the window one width of a cill,
crunches the outside air like an apple,
rubs circulation in his dried fruit fingers.
His flesh camouflages the neighbour's *cheval de frise*.

Like Nelson at Trafalgar Square he stands on a box,
a *cache-sex* of foam still glistening,
a ripple in the bath-water where his body was,
the tidemark he'd been taught to clean unscoured.

And like the boy in the fairy tale
he sees the room in emperor's clothes.

PREVIOUS ADDRESSEE

Readdressed in his best Sunday script
he drops off her mail at the main post branch –
sub-branches for bills of course –
and in doing for her thus he feels they are related: tenants-in-law,
and adds her name to his mailing list
of nieces nephews cousins once or twice removed

he pieces together a jigsaw of her identikit
in her time the room was kosher
she restored paintings at the Tate
was half-Greek half-Spanish
he got that from the pictures on the stamps
alabaster adobe houses and cerulean sky

an old man peers up at the skylight,
the studios along the row are dark,
and watches the sun laser through the missing pieces of leaves –
there's no more correspondence in his tray.

SMALL IS BEAUTIFUL

He likes:
the smallness of the exhibition,
the little children with their parents
even if they do slow down his way
of seeing things in quick time.

the way they talk,
their speech bubbles party balloons
tied to the gateposts of grand houses.

the programme,
'Lady Mouse in Mob Cap', which he decides
to send to a niece in Gloucester.

his lunch at the coffee shop;
smoked trout followed by good yoghurt,
then coffee with milk and brown sugar
still crystallised from being in the fridge
and which he has to crack like an eggshell.

He is careful, outside in the street,
not to walk on the cracks in the pavement
even if it does slow people down.

QUARTER CENTURY CLUB

Trees have been knee-capped in the storm
and need the hand of healing:
some have been pulled up like dahlias
others bow down their broken stacks.

My uncle goes to his Quarter Century Club
(sounds like a Sherlock Holmes mystery)
serving members and non-serving members
of twenty-five years standing and above.

He finds the restaurant has been done up:
tarot cards swirling on the walls
like those saucy pictures
which added spice to the food.

The restaurant is crowded:
he views the backs of heads
with gibbous moons of baldness showing
through the stitchery of scalps.

He walks to the World's End Post Office:
autumn has been repealed
at the snap of one night's fingers –
he finds waiting for him poste restante

a Jane Avril postcard from his step-niece:
Jane Avril! A thing of beauty!
Was the artist not a cripple?
Like all the crippled trees of London.

COBELLIGERENT

We watched him waving,
shadowly visible through his glass front-door,
like one of those generals tracked down
by TV cameras.

Cardiganed in old age,
lips blue as Tiptree's blueberry jam,
he looked through a family
wedding album with us.

'Your brother takes a good photo,'
he said of one of the few people
that he knew. *'Looking more
and more like his father.'*

I lobbed some words at him: *Rome,
Naples, Milan* which he played with a straight bat
and *Italians* which got *'cobelligerents'*,
a half-chance I put down.

Clearer than any wedding
photograph I see him
darkly through a glass-door
which he closed on me. On war.

FOOTNOTE TO HISTORY

Something my cousin said,
some footnote to history
like the Christmas truce in World War One.
Some story about my uncle's minder
taking him for a drink
on their way back from the prison hospital.

But what amazed my cousin was
the German had un-strapped his gun-belt
and left it suspended from a hook.
Imagine the shadowy-lit interior
with its single bulb
like a moon three days shy of full,

the fug of fifty brands of smoke
pressing on the imprisoned air.
Imagine the double helix
from the cigarettes of friend and foe,
and the amber mugs of beer
shoulder to shoulder on the bar.

And hanging heavy in their cups,
the holstered guns at the edge
of the room. At the edge of my uncle's eye.

ON THE TROOPSHIP

Magnificent old seadog
with a shock of white hair
and grizzled growth of beard –
birds die on the wing like benedictions
as we   oat over your pages
and pull out strings and strings
of your carrier bags like magicians.

Was that you
in your dark Rasputin cloak
on the troopship *Drottingholm*?
I hope you had a fair journey then
in the teeth of the storm
for I know what it's like, that *soubade*,
that heartfelt sickness for home.

This time it's not the Swedish-American line
and it's the boatman who's hooded and cloaked.

THE WELSH POX

Although my uncle was an away supporter
of Theatr Clwyd and knew by heart
the whole of Fluellen's part in *Henry the Fifth*
I never caught him quoting
from *Under Milk Wood* in a sacerdotal voice.

Although my uncle always wore a daffodil
and consumed a leek on St David's Day

I never caught him stealing to chapel
or applying for membership
of a Male Voice Choir.

Being Welsh wasn't the cause of his death.
Only rumour has it the vaccination
on his arm had the template of dragons.

CHARTER PARTY

It's as if you'd just slipped out.
Your metal mirror with lines
of copperplate condensation.
Your socks. Prewar. Heather.
With a 'School for the Blind' label.
Your swaggerstick with silver motto:
Mens agitat molem. Mind over matter.
Your poor man's bible of postcards
from visits to the National Gallery.

The personal correspondence. A copy
of a letter you wrote with apologies
for writing 'instead of one of my sisters'.
Rugby injuries. An arm that had to be re-set
'massaged by one of the school sergeants'.
War wounds. Your refusal to work for those who
'registered puppet companies abroad
to avoid their fair burden of taxation'.

We try to read the script: ship's disbursements,
bills of lading, the official form of charter parties.
Add our own comment to your 'cooked'
retirement card. 'Much missed by all.'

We pick up one of your socks. Erase
the ledger headings of condensation
from the mirror like a magic pad.
Then blow on it a film of living breath.

The sun burns ice-stubble on the window-pane,
trees grow inside out in the Churchillian
cold. There is no more matter over mind.

AT THE CREMATORIUM

We want to wave like Sir Bedivere
as the coffin eases its shoulders
through the curtained hatchway
then gathers knots and disappears
beyond the empty slipway.

We ease back into the saddle
hitching up what's left of our courage.

TONTINE

One thing we said about him:
he walked barefoot up Moel Famma.
Another, his fierce independent spirit
would send presents back to sender.

We remember the red ace blemish on his forehead
when he went to hospital in a taxi
like Noel Coward in pyjamas,
dressing gown and slippers.

'Look! No relations!' as though proud
of this logistic conjuring trick.
Those were his greener years.

Now it's us leaving memories on the collection plate
like stakes in a game of cards:
Survivor takes all.

Like Dürer's or Rodin's *Hands of God*
our praying hands grow inches longer
and a part of us shivers
extravagantly in the cold.

THE PRISONER

French windows give onto a runway of lawn.
Lefthand fence mufti'd in winter jasmine.
A few weeds have made a break for it
behind the Anderson shelter.

Inside is the Sunday finish of china,
the polished knobbliness of staircases.
Smells strike the hours. Toast, hot milk, shoe polish
and three reeks a day of lamb's liver catfood.
There's a whiff of tea caddies and travellers' tales.

Hygienic gloves hang on hooks for removing
the reinforced rubber lids of dustbins.
A J-cloth for wiping milk bottles
and their tiny plastic baseball caps;
the milk is isolated in the fridge
in separate blood groups.

Even the cat has special cartons.
Only the cat is allowed to leave pawprints
on the kitchen table. Even a burglar
would have to brush his feet at the door
or take a turn with the Ewbank.

Mountain ash sends out long beggarly shoots.
The wrought iron gates shut to
in uncomfortable wedlock. Between them
a metal stake cocks a sharp snook at the world.